60 Dates
in Six Months
WITH A BROKEN NECK

Maureen Anne Meehan

60 Dates in Six Months (with a Broken Neck)
Copyright © 2024 by Maureen Anne Meehan

ISBN: 978-1639459254(hc)
ISBN: 978-1639459230(sc)
ISBN: 978-1639459247(e)

Writers' Branding
(877) 608-6550
www.writersbranding.com
media@writersbranding.com

Table of Contents

Preface

My husband passed away after a gallant battle with a rare cancer ten years ago, and it left us and our four children devastated. On the final week of our time together (while driving home from the DMV to get car title changes to minimize chaos after his certain death), he told me that he loved me dearly and that he wanted me to find love again. He was such a giving soulmate. We fell in love by accident. We were both avid runners in the early hours of each day, and one dark winter morning, I literally ran into to him on our running loops. I knew him as he lived nearby, was a lawyer as well, and our boys were in the same preschool. He told me that he didn't feel that it was safe for me to run alone in the dark, so he asked that we meet at the same street corner in the morning and run our loop together. I agreed. We ran every weekday together for years as friends. We conversed with ease about any subject, and we had a lot of friends and colleagues in common.

One morning he shocked me and gave me a kiss at the end of the run. I felt our energy building for months, but I didn't want to make the first move. He was a late bloomer, and it took him a long time to gather the nerve to kiss me. And we were married to other people. Neither of us were happily married, and we spoke of it often. I had decided to leave my marriage. It was over. But he was afraid to leave his despite its lacking love because he worried about giving up time with his boys. I didn't want to influence him one way or another with his choice. I was moving forward with mine and I did.

He painfully vacillated his decision, but ultimately chose to leave a terrible marriage. We both had messy divorces. Rumors flew in our community about our affair, and it affected all four of our kids, which was extremely difficult to endure. We fought hard and moved mountains to be together and ultimately prevailed on creating our Brady Bunch. Our kids remain extremely close to this day. We married and went on a familymoon to London and France. It was a blast. Our new life took on another meaning, but it wasn't without some growing pains.

When we learned of his cancer diagnosis not long after our marriage in 2009, we swiftly searched for solutions. We went to chemo and radiation appointments together, and he was rarely without me during treatment. It was an arduous four years of chasing remedies, and our careers certainly made our time limited, but more importantly, making sure that our collective children were getting their needs met. That took a village of family and friends, and for that, I am forever grateful.

We learned eventually that the word *terminal* is not a place at the airport. It was real, and it was certain. No matter what we did. We are both marathoners, so informing us that the finish line was just changed was unheard of for us. But it was happening. And it did. He passed away in 2014 at our home, and it was beyond the worst thing that has ever happened to us. The kids were luckily asleep in the middle of the night when he passed. But they awoke to a very quiet home and they knew. His last words to them on the day before his passing was to make him proud. All four of them have honored their promise to him.

It has taken me a long time to grieve him, but I finally did with the help of therapy in 2023. I am grateful to my therapist who had no problem laughing and crying with me every week. She has changed my life and my perspective on letting go. It was time to move forward.

I told her toward the end of 2023 that my 2024 motto was to "say yes" and to "hold my halo." I started dating in November 2023. It's been awful. Dating in your fifties in Orange County, California, is not for the faint of heart.

I didn't venture out with the idea of writing a novel. I ventured to find love. By the title of this nonfiction satire, I found a whole lot of things quite shy of love. And so it begins: *60 Dates in Six Months (with a Broken Neck)*.

Goodbye Coffee

I met a nice man through a Catholic single website, and after the usual texts and finally an agreement to exchange cell phone numbers, we started chatting. He was a divorced father of two adult boys, and he was genuinely a vice nice guy. We agreed to meet for a hike. and we ended up walking for hours on the beach and connected instantly. I told him my story about losing my husband and he cried—real tears while staring at me and listening intently.

We hiked a few more times in November, and we seemed to be getting along very well. It was closing in on my birthday, and he invited me to dinner. He brought me flowers. We had a great meal and shared entrees and a bottle of wine. He walked me to my car and gave me a soft kiss. He checked to make sure that I got home safely and was absolutely a gentleman.

We continued down this path for a bit, but he never had time to get together because he was always at the church. Perhaps he should have been a "man of the cloth," I don't know. But I made my intentions clear that while my faith is a very important part of my life, that dating and finding love again was my goal.

He didn't make time for me. I wasn't impressed, and I'm not shy about sharing my feelings. He didn't care for it.

He accused me of being jealous of his time at the church. I accused him of using the "Holy Ghost" as a reason to not pick up the pace a little.

I was not in a hurry, but I didn't want to be his last priority either, and that was how I felt, and I wasn't shy about telling him so. That didn't go over very well.

After a few days of not hearing from him, he asked me to meet him for coffee. I agreed. I spent time picking out a darling casual outfit and made myself look desirable. I was punctual as always. He was late as usual. He was offended that I ordered my own coffee and was waiting for him. He then proceeded to tell me that I am intimidating because I did the Hawaii Ironman Triathlon. I said, "Thirty years ago?" Yes, that intimidated him. I'd done countless marathons. Poor thing. I was also a professional woman with a good career and the mother of four wonderful adult children. There was such a laundry list of intimidations that I just decided to not inundate him with my greatness. I've worked hard for them, and a man should be proud and admire a tenacious hardworking woman.

I decided that it wasn't worth my time. I thanked him for his and I left.

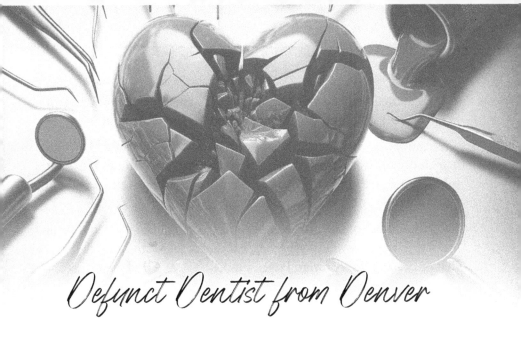

Defunct Dentist from Denver

He was exceptionally handsome and outdoorsy and athletic with a toned physique. He was also a dentist, and I come from a family of dentists, so we immediately had a lot to talk about. He was an avid skier as am I and loved to ski at the same places I matriculate. What could go wrong? We could meet in Colorado at a resort on our mutual ski pass and start this blissful journey showing off to each other on the ski slopes. Wrong.

These dating apps allow first names only, so it takes using the app to get a cell phone number to text and eventually call. But if one is going to meet someone else, it is prudent to get a last name to check them out to ensure that they are not a career criminal serial killer.

As we got closer to thinking about meeting in Colorado, he gave me his last name. Google is a helpful friend. She knows where to look.

As I honed in on his three dental offices, she (Google) pointed out that none of them were his dental practices any longer. They had been sold to other dentists.

She then pointed out that his dad was a dentist and might have sold a few practices in Chicago.

She then pointed me in the direction of litigation for ethics violations and that not only had his dad lost his license to practice, he had as well.

The dental practices had been sold for judgment debts from litigation for malpractice for him (in Colorado) and his father (in Illinois).

I called him and we talked for hours about this situation. He painted it with broad strokes and Monet colors. It was a good thing. He made a lot of money selling these thriving practices. He's semi-retired and got a lot of good powder on the slopes.

I should be so lucky to be considering dating him. I was not feeling lucky. I felt like I was in Vegas at a blackjack table with roulette players. Red or Black. Odd or Even. Pretty simple choices. Hard pass.

All Dressed Up and Nowhere to Go

VP high end executive pharma guy who was stunningly handsome and lived in picturesque Corona del Mar a few miles up the beach from me. He had one daughter, and he seemed to prioritize her more than his own life, which I truly appreciate.

We met over the holidays, and he was on a ski trip with his daughter. He took her to four great destinations that I love and that were on our ski pass. We kept in touch a little and then a lot, and he sent me selfies of him and his adorable daughter. He was going to be gone with her through the new year, so we agreed that when school resumed for her, we would meet. We both worked from home, and we were only a few miles away from one another. It was exhilarating.

And then I fell in my kitchen and broke my neck. I will be honest about how it happened. My girlfriends and I had Costco coupons for a local good restaurant, and they announced that they were shuttering after decades in business. We needed to use our coupon. We met on a Friday for happy hour and proceeded to have three martinis each with appetizers. By the time our dinners arrived, it was time to go to bed. Too much, too early with not enough food.

One of their husbands picked us up and drove us home and walked us to our respective doors with our take-home dinners untouched.

I went to bed at nine. I don't drink martinis. I'm thin. Not enough food.

I awoke at four in the morning starving. The kind of starving that you are not getting back to sleep. The alcohol sugar had burned off, and the body needed what it needed. I went down to my kitchen like a ravenous raccoon and grabbed the salmon leftovers to heat up in the microwave. I then went to get my Sriracha in the fridge to properly heat my salmon that was dry, and I missed the handle to the refrigerator door and I fell backward with velocity onto my travertine kitchen floor.

I awoke an hour or so later and I could smell blood. I tried to reach back to feel the back of my head, but my right arm was immobile.

I reached back with my left arm, and I felt a pool of blood.

I needed to call an ambulance. My cell was upstairs on my nightstand. I knew I had a broken neck. I couldn't move.

It took me an hour and a half to try to turn over and crawl upstairs with a broken neck and no use in my right arm.

Luckily, my phone charger was a long cable, and I was able to pull it off my nightstand. I called 911. I told dispatch that I broke my neck. They questioned me about my certainty about the diagnosis. I explained that I had scoliosis and that I had my spine fused from the tip of my neck to my tailbone, and I could tell that my neck was broken. They asked if I had a spare key to enter my home and I explained that my house had been broken into in July 2023 by gang members and I had been robbed, so there was no key outside. (Note: the gang broke a window in my bathroom and stole my jewelry, etc., and my pillowcase to carry my belongings and it had nothing to do with a spare key, but I digress.)

I was able to sled myself headfirst down my staircase and let the emergency response team in. They were gracious enough to grab my purse and wrap me in a blanket since I'd lost my pajama bottoms on the way down the staircase.

They promised to shut the door so that my rescue kittens did not get out.

It was confirmed that my neck was badly shattered in two places and that there was spinal cord damage. All I could hear from the trauma team was quadriplegic.

I knew I was in trouble. I called my son in Tucson and told him he needed to drive home because he was my logistically closest child with my authority under my healthcare directive. He agreed.

I met my stunningly gorgeous neurosurgeon before surgery, and he showed me the MRI of my broken neck. It was ugly. I asked him to direct his trauma team to stop saying quadriplegic. I wanted to ski at Deer Valley in March or April (this was January 6, 2024). He smirked and told me that this was a severe fracture and that we would take this a day at a time.

I then proceeded to tell him how to do the surgery since I had scoliosis and was fused from my neck to my tailbone by a world-renowned orthopedic surgeon in LA. He knew my surgeon well and smirked again. He promised to take good care of me.

When I awoke from the procedure, he was there. This beautiful man. He showed me the X-ray, and I complimented his work. He was pleased.

He saved my life.

I could move my arms and legs. I had gross motor deficit to my right arm, but everything else was good. I was not a quadriplegic.

After seeing him in the ICU for five days, I told him that I needed to go home to heal. I needed rest and proper nutrition and that I would discharge AMA (against medical advice). He thought I was crazy. But he knew I knew my rights. He signed the form.

On the way out, I asked if he was single (reminder that he's stunning). He said that his wife would kill him. I told him that she had good taste. So this chapter isn't about him.

It's about the executive pharma guy with the daughter on a ski trip. My son had to take my phone and cancel a few dates already set up prior to my accident. Of course, my daughter would have offered details. My son just told these guys that I had to cancel because I broke my neck.

I'm sure these guys thought that the excuse was original. People cancel willy nilly in this world without explanation.

This was truthful. But it wasn't accompanied by elaboration. In our new dating world, no one cares unfortunately.

When I got home from the hospital and finally refused medication and got to the business of healing. I looked at the communications from my son to a few guys, and I realized I needed to do some damage control. I reached out to explain. To their credit, all three men were great.

Atlanta had already moved to his new job. Retired Hot Fireman Ghost had met someone else. But All Dressed Up with Nowhere to Go was still on his trip with his daughter, so we hadn't skipped a beat.

He came to my house two days after I was discharged from the ICU. We had a glass of wine and talked for hours. Kissed passionately. He had to pick her up from her Friday night art class and he left late to get her.

I was a jerk and a few days later told him he was too Newport for me and not enough Wyoming.

But I remained enamored. I reached out a month later and apologized. We met for lunch at a great place in Corona del Mar on a Friday and had lunch. It was great.

He told me about his business trip to Nashville the following week, and we agreed to have dinner the following Monday night prior to his departure on Tuesday morning.

I got ready. If you are reading this: a woman closing in on sixty getting ready for a date is serious business. The hair. Makeup. Wardrobe choices and changes to the wardrobe choices. It's hours of preparation and anticipation.

We confirmed Monday morning. He had a busy day preparing for his work trip Tuesday. Once he was done working, he was to text me where to meet and what time.

All Dressed Up with Nowhere to Go. He ghosted me.

It was January in Southern California, and I lived a mile from the coast. It gets cold at night. Moist ocean onflow wet cold. I had agreed to meet an engineer who loves to ski and run at 180 Blu at the Ritz Carlton. It's a mile from my house. May I remind you that it's cold once the sun sets.

I showed up in cute "boyfriend" jeans and a tank with a blazer and awesome boots. The bar overlooked to Pacific Ocean. It had heaters. But it was cold at night. They even had fuzzy blanket for the ladies. I'd seen a few blokes bundled up.

I arrived punctually as per my norm. He was punctual too. But he was overweight.

We ordered wine. Me, Pinor Noir Red Blend Napa. Him, a buttery Chardonnay. Who cares?

We proceed to converse, but his first question was: "Where is your LBD?" I had no idea what this bellybush was asking me.

I asked for clarification, and he explained that his ladies wore little black dresses for the first date.

I reminded him that it was January over the Pacific, and it was cold, but we couldn't relate.

I asked him about running since we matched because he is a "runner," but it turned out that he only runs to the fridge.

I asked about his skiing, but it turned out that he tried once and didn't take to it.

But he took to his buttery chardonnay in fifteen minutes. He excused himself to the restroom, and I pleaded with our lovely host for the check. He said that he ordered another buttery Chard.

I asked him to put it on my tab. I paid cash and ran to valet.

I'd already warned these nice young men that it was a blind date and begged to leave my car out front. They were kind.

End of LBD.

PF Changs

It seems like there are a lot of engineers on these dating apps. Intelligence is important to me so that's attractive, and let's face it, if you are in your fifties or sixties and looks are everything, you are going to be sorely disappointed.

Men are bald with bellies. Women have had the ultimate hell of menopause. Gaining weight because you thought about dinner. It is bad. I can't lie about it.

But I connected with an engineer who lived within reasonable dating range, and we went for a hike, and he didn't drop dead.

I choose hikes for a start to make sure I'm not the "Nurse with a Purse" for the guy who is going to stroke out in my bed.

We'd gone on a hike. We decided for a future date. We agreed he would pick me up after I had explained that I'd prefer to just meet. I'm a good driver from Wyoming, for God's sake.

Anyhow, he arrived late. I'd opened a beautiful Austin Hope red blend. It's been breathing. He arrived empty handed. No flowers. No wine. No game. But he brought his big belly.

He liked a buttery Chardonnay. I had a bestie that likes that, so I crack a good one from Daou. He chugged with abandon. It's now time for dinner.

He wants to go to PF Chang's. It's a fine chain, don't get me wrong. But we have awesome variety in Laguna. Going to the mall is not the thing

I recommend a local award-winning Chinese a mile away. It's not his plan. He knows PF Chang's. He's out of his zone. He pouted. But we went to my local mom and pop. He loved it. He took the leftovers of my order. The End.

French Sushi

Good looking and athletic and divorced with daughters in high school. It's livable, I guess.

We agreed based on a thirty-minute commute that we would simply meet for dinner. We both loved sushi. I had a favorite place down the street. We could meet.

We did meet. He's still handsome, but his pictures were old. He was weathered, but it was not the worst. Hint: I will describe the worst later.

We met at the local sushi place. It's small but wonderful with horrible logistics, and we had gone there as a family multiple times. We celebrated my late husband's birthday there. It was our jam.

Until I met French Sushi.

We met for dinner. We sat at the sushi bar. We ordered drinks and a lot of sashimi. We were both athletic, and protein was our thing.

I had my first bite of salmon sashimi, and he French-kissed me. At the sushi bar. The one I go to with my kids. The one I know all of my neighbors of twenty-six years.

I had to relocate to a new sushi bar.

I'm sorry, Jizake. Thank you to Dana Kai for your kindness.

I take myself on a date after church on Sunday night to Dana Kai. It's often my only date of the week. But it is reliable.

May I Sell Your House guru

This is a peculiar tale. I grew up in Sheridan, Wyoming, which is a Western darling quintessential town on a famous Rodeo circuit with a significant Rodeo purse. It is a gigantic part of my soul. It is my hometown.

Enter Guru OC. I was having dinner with my girlfriend who had now lived in Australia with her hubby of thirty-five years.

I set them up on a blind date. I met her in grad school in San Diego. She was a fashionable La Jolla girl getting her master's degree in education for a bump in salary for retirement.

I met her. She was gorgeous and grew up in La Jolla. She had fashion and sorority sisters. I wore Moccasins and had two jobs and going to school.

We became best friends.

I was dating a guy (that's always how a gal's story goes) and she had just gone through a bad breakup. She had cool friends with cool fashions, and I was a dork from Wyo without fashion. She took me under her wing.

The guy I was dating loved to sail. His bestie loved to sail. They were racing that weekend out of Oceanside Harbor on a thirty-foot. They needed some weight. My guy asked me if I had a friend. I said that I only had one friend in San Diego. He asked me to invite her. I did. She said yes.

She managed to barf the entire time on the regatta. Not a good show.

We were staying at a seedy Costa Mesta drive in. The noises next door were epic.

They have been married for thirty-five years and live in Australia with their two adult children.

Meanwhile, I remain single.

But back to him.

I was with my Australian (now) girlfriend who married to Aussie Bloke despite all. She and I meet for travel all over the world.

She was in the US and was staying with me. I took her to my new local fav a mile away, Botegga Angelina. We were on the patio having a cocktail, and Guru asked if he could take our picture. We agreed.

Guru gave me his biz card.

I contacted Guru. I had known him for thirty years, but he was too much of a dumbass to connect the dots.

I lighted him up.

He came over for leftovers. I literally asked him for leftovers, and he was excited. He proceeded to take a self-guided tour of my house and commented on its selling points as he was the area real estate guru. He proceeded on his self-tour.

He analyzed the good and bad and ugly.

My house was not for sale.

Meaty Mits

Wen agreed to meet for a hike on the Salt Creek Trail near my house. He lived only a few miles away, and he'd not walked on this trail. That should have been my clue.

We met early in the morning, and it was chilly, and luckily, I had my hoodie. He didn't need a hoodie. He was grossly overweight. He described himself as "fit." and I quickly was realizing that this term was obscure.

He was nice and conversive, and we had a relatively good time for two hours walking and talking. We walked to Salt Creek Beach and then Strands Beach, and I showed him the cool beach shack that has great food and cocktails for amazing sunsets. Again, he lived a few miles away, and he's never heard of this shack.

I walk or hike nearly every day, and including dating in this realm was new. But I was going to walk or hike anyway, and I am a multitasker, so this made perfect sense to me. Get to know the guy doing what you were going to be doing anyway. If it doesn't work out, who cares? You got your steps in.

But I wasn't prepared to accept Meaty Mits. He was humongous, and his hands were the size of my head. I'm not super judgmental, but I believe that I did emphasize that fitness is a huge part of my life in my dating profile. He wasn't fit. His hands were gigantic. And all I could think about was not having them touch my body.

At the end of the hike, he walked me to the gate to my community on the Salt Creek Trail. I was never so grateful for living in this community with a guard and a gate. He was never entering.

I know the guards at both gates by name. I stop and talk with them regularly. I make them cookies at Christmas. I do this because that is the right thing to do. On this day, it paid off. Meaty Mits wanted me to invite him to my home for "breakfast." I'm pretty sure that the guard was picking up on what was going down. This guy with giant hands grabbed my face to kiss me, and I felt like he was going to swallow me whole. Luckily the guard interrupted this scene.

I galloped through the gate and never looked back.

Atlanta

He lives in Newport Beach. I'm in South Laguna area. Why not meet at Starbucks at Laguna Main Beach for an early cup of coffee before a hike? Sounds like a good plan.

He's a widower. I'm a widow. We've both been dealt a bad hand. He's fit and gorgeous and smart. Maybe this is my lucky day.

He had ordered my coffee, and we were sitting by the window overlooking Main Beach. It was an unusually high surf, and the waves were breaking over the boardwalk, so we were not going to be able to walk the beach. Plan B would be Heisler Park, which was equally lovely.

We enjoyed hours of walking and talking. He's an engineer working on a major project at a local hotel. It's been a controversial issue regarding the modernization of this landmark in Laguna and the subject of much litigation. He's in the thick of it and was tired of the delays that this controversy had caused. He had two kids in college and had decided that collegiate tuition was going to be an issue, so he had decided to accept a position in Atlanta that paid more. His kids were young adults, and he could move for employment.

I am not one for long distance relationships. They are challenging. I am impatient.

I wish he would have told me on the phone. I would have skipped over this chapter. He was fit and handsome and smart and moving to Atlanta, Georgia.

That wasn't going to work for me.

Don't Tell Me What to Do. You are Not My Cat

He lived in Aliso Viejo near one of my favorite wilderness parks where I go for long and arduous hikes. I wanted to go for a hike, and I explained on the phone that my favorite trails are hiking up Choya and hiking down Mathis. It's a six miler with a nine-hundred-foot elevation gain. It's a good workout. He's fit and he could handle it.

And then I told him that I have a broken neck.

My mistake. He proceeded to tell me that I need time to heal and that when I am healed, we can make a plan. I held my breath and didn't say the thought bubble that's about to burst. Read the title to this chapter. But I was a mature adult woman and didn't retaliate. I just listened to this stranger tell me what I needed.

Fast-forward a month and he reached out to inquire of my health status. You can't unbreak your neck. I'm fused from my neck to my tailbone as the result of scoliosis. It's a gift that keeps on giving. My neck was inevitable. It was planned to be fused in 2020, but I had already been under the knife for too long and my orthopedic surgeon opted to finish the spine and plan the neck for a different day. We didn't expect me to fall in my kitchen and break it. But that's life. It can be unexpected at times. I'm lucky to be alive.

But if I tell you I am worthy of a good hike, please don't tell me that I'm not. You are not my cat.

I'm a forgiving creature, and I agreed to go for this hike on a Saturday. He had an electrician coming on Saturday, so he's not sure about his window of opportunity. He would text me a time.

He didn't. I woke up on Sunday to a text from him asking, "Is today our day?" I responded that yesterday was our day.

31 is not the new 51

His picture depicted a darling man in his ski goggles on a bluebird day on the slopes. I am hyper focused on meeting someone who enjoys the same activities. I taught my late husband to ski. I taught his boys to ski. You need to be on the slopes with me to date me.

He called one evening to set up a ski date. Turned out he was a snowboarder, so that was a challenge as I wanted to go to Deer Valley where snowboarding was not allowed.

As we continued to talk, he sounded generationally young. I asked him how old he was. He admitted that he's thirty-one. Not fifty-one like he advertised on the dating app. He asked if that was a problem. I confirmed that it was a major unsurmountable obstacle since my oldest son was twenty-nine. End of story.

Swiftie

This is going to be a short chapter. The dating app asks what type of music one likes. I like pretty much all genres, and since I'm from Wyoming, I love country and country rock—including Taylor Swift who might be more pop country at the moment, but I love her. I love her stories and her tenacity and her boldness and her marketing genius. I know the names of her cats. Meredith, Olivia and Benjamin.

He hated her and told me he's disinterested in me because I'm a Swiftie. Deal breaker.

Chico Lit Up

He went to Colorado State University at the same time my sister and I did. It's a big school, and he's an agriculture major, and I was in the business school, so if we crossed paths, I would not have noticed. I would have been speeding on my bike to class.

He's Irish. I'm Irish. He loves to ski as do I. He's in the fertilizer business in Chico which is a good business. His favorite place to ski is Breckenridge in Colorado. I've been with my Irish family to Breckenridge many times, and it's a good mountain.

He had access to a private plane, and he's going to fly down to see me, but it was raining cats and dogs, and he's literally shoveling shit into sandbags. Rivers were overflowing their banks, and he's trying to save his business and help others do the same. He's unable to fly. That's fine. I understand that life can sometimes get in the way. I'm not worried, but please just communicate the problem. My husband was ill for years and I had four teenagers at the time, and we had to cancel often due to unforeseen circumstances. But just communicate. That's all I ask.

That was apparently a major problem for Chico Lit Up, and he had an Irish temper that surpassed mine. End of story. He had the last word.

Debbie Downer

He's my age and had a good job as an engineer for Chevron and loved to ski. He had two daughters and one son, and they were grown and had flown the coop. He had time and opportunity to have some fun. I was ready.

We decided to talk instead of text. He's the most negative and flat-toned person I'd ever communicated with. Everything was bleak. His job was awful and his kids didn't keep in touch and his ex-wife hated him. Sound like fun yet? I wouldn't know. I had to go do something. Anything. Other than him.

Is This How it Ends?

He's a CPA in San Diego with a good, steady job and a twenty-five-year-old son who was out of college and on his own. He loves to ski. He loves to hike, and he actually is fit.

He suggested meeting at a trailhead in Carlsbad as it was a halfway meeting point. He sent me a pin to the trail, and it was in a nice residential area near a nice resort, and I had friends who live nearby this trail in case there was a problem.

Turned out that this trail to the Eucalyptus Grove dead-ended into what appeared to be a cult fort where teenagers do weird things. I wish I would have taken a picture of what was there because I couldn't do it justice with words. There were the usual empty beer cans and vodka bottles. One would expect that. But there was a fire ring filled with other sacrificial tokens. And the picnic table had demonic masks nailed to it. Similar masks were dangling from trees. I felt like I was in a *Silence of the Lambs* scene and this was where I lay to rot. My daughter knew where I was hiking, but she lived on the East Coast, so it's going to take time for her to find my rotting corpse. I'd come to terms with it. It was a dead end to this trail. It's all making sense.

He's a good sport when I told him that I was seriously uncomfortable and that I wanted to turn around and head back. We did. He agreed that we can just walk the neighborhood and run into neighbors walking their dogs and riding bikes with their kids. We had great conversation. It's a gorgeous day. But I couldn't do this again. He's the Cult Guy.

Cheer Dad

I was at Orange County airport going through security en route to meet friends in Las Vegas for the U2 concert at the Sphere. The concert was incredible, and the forum was highly recommended.

I was waiting for my puffy jacket at security as the girls behind me had placed their backpack on it. I was listening to these preteen girls talk about their designer hair gel and makeup, and my thought bubble was "only in Orange County."

I texted my girlfriend who was also en route to Las Vegas in the car and told her about these girls who were likely going to Vegas for a cheer competition. I had noted that Cheer Dad was handsome and designer label as well. Cheer Mom showed up a little later, and she too was well kempt.

It was a Southwest Airlines flight, so open seating. The three girls were on one side of the aisle, and mom and dad on the other, so I asked if I could join them. They agreed.

We started visiting, and I was telling mom about the book I was writing, and Cheer Dad leaned in and suggested that I date him. You can imagine my thought bubble. Turned out that they were divorced and in unison to support their girls. Cool. Mom suggested that I give my number to Cheer Dad. I asked him his age. Forty-seven. I was fifty-eight and thinking that

I was too old for him. Apparently that was not the case. He gave me his number in front of his ex-wife. She asked for my number as well.

We were one big happy family. But I lost my phone at the Sphere and that was the end of that.

Psychedelic Hiker

I'd set up a hiking date with a very handsome fella from Laguna Beach. We agreed to meet at the Main Beach lighthouse on noon on a Saturday. It was a beautiful day.

We had not exchanged cell phones yet, so the only way to communicate was via the app. I don't check the app often, but that morning, I luckily did. He had cancelled the hike. His reasoning was that he'd been up until five in the morning doing psychedelic drugs and that he was too out of it to hike. Hard pass on that.

I went hiking with a couple from my neighborhood and told them about it. We laughed. Dodged another bullet.

I got back from the hike and checked the app, and he had reached back out saying that he was feeling a little better and could meet me. It was past noon and I'd already hiked. I didn't respond. He then reached out again offering his cell. Again, pass.

Cheesecake Guy

This high-end businessman who was raised in Oklahoma but had lived in Texas spotted my eye. He was handsome and exceptionally bright. We talked on the phone a few times and agreed to meet for dinner at the Spectrum, which is an outdoor popular mall in Irvine.

He suggested a nice restaurant called Del Frisco and we had a nice dinner. Turned out that he'd gone to maximum effort to go on the date because he had spent the day in the ER with dizzy spells. They'd run all kinds of tests on him, and they were not sure the cause.

Now I was worried that he's going to keel over on our date of a stroke or heart attack, so I suggested that we eat at the bar so that there were witnesses.

The date went nicely, and he asked me out again for dinner for the next week. I agreed.

He suggested the Cheesecake Factory, which wasn't too impressive with the variety of choice in Orange County, and I teased him that it would take me all night to rifle through the thirty-six-page menu.

Since I'd driven to him the week prior, we agreed to meet in the middle, and there is a Cheesecake Factory in Mission Viejo. I showed up on time as I am punctual and texted that I was walking in. He said that he was in the lobby area waiting. I didn't see him.

He called me and asked me which Cheescake Factory I was in and I explained. He told me that he was in the Spectrum mall one. I reminded him that we had agreed to meet in the middle. It was raining. He didn't have his car. I'm not an unreasonable person, so I agreed to drive to him in the rain. I did.

We had dinner, and when it was time to pay the bill, he was extremely precise with our waiter about how he wanted his card run. There was some kind of miscommunication, and it was not handled according to his instructions.

He threw a fit and demanded to see the manager. She approached, and he dressed her down with utter disdain. I was mortified. People were staring.

I finally excused myself and took a twenty-dollar bill out of my wallet and tracked down the waiter to ensure that he was tipped. I then proceeded to my car.

He came running out after me apologizing profusely for his rude behavior. I acknowledged him and kept walking. He followed me to my car and then proceeded to ask me for a ride home. It was raining.

I'm not heartless, so I gave him a ride to his corporate housing high-rise nearby. He then asked if I wanted to go upstairs and see his apartment. I passed.

Shiver Me Timbers

I connected with a handsome guy who lived on the Island of Catalina, which is about 30 nautical miles west of Dana Point. He suggested that we meet for lunch. He had his own sailboat. He suggested that I take the Catalina Express boat to meet him on Catalina.

Did I mention that he had his own boat?

Metrosexual Grammy Guy

I had been talking on the phone for days with this extremely gorgeous anesthesiologist from Newport Beach who also was a Grammy-nominated musician. Talk about left and right brain. I was of course very intrigued.

We had agreed to meet for a hike in the Back Bay of Newport Beach on a Saturday. He told me that he had a deadline to finish a score (music) and that he'd let me know when he was done.

He kept delaying the time by a few hours until the point that it was getting late in the day. I'd already gone hiking by then. He suggested dinner instead, and being flexible, I agreed. I went to church, and then we met halfway at a new restaurant in Aliso Viejo.

There was a little traffic, and he was a few minutes late but called me en route with his ETA. When he arrived, he was dressed to the nines and looked stunning. I brought a nice bottle of wine with me, and we shared the bottle and shared a few entrees. Everything was going well, but I noticed that he kept looking at himself in the mirror behind me. I didn't think much of it.

He was going to visit one of his six children the next week, so he asked if we could go out again the following week. I agreed. I never heard from him again.

Commit to Me

I spoke on the phone for hours upon hours to a gentleman who lived in Utah. We had a lot in common, and he loves to ski. He has two adult sons who are educated and independent, and his ex-wife remarried and moved back to Mexico, so she wasn't going to be an issue.

We had planned on meeting in Utah to go skiing, but the snow was not ideal yet. He's retired and owns residential apartments, so his passive income provided him a very nice lifestyle.

He was in Sacramento for a basketball game and wanted to see if he could fly from Sacramento and meet up in San Diego. It was very spur of the moment, and I was new to how this dating thing worked. Nervous about making such a big commitment, I told him that I needed to think it over for a few days. He took this pregnant pause as extreme rejection and yelled at me. Note that I have never met him in person, and I don't like to be bullied and yelled at. Who does?

If you yell at me, you are out. So Utah is out.

Keep the Boots On

In a few of the photos that I have posted on the app, I am wearing a variety of boots. I'm from Wyoming, so boots are a natural fit. And I have an excellent collection of boots and booties.

In one picture I am wearing my Bad Boss Bitch Boots. My daughter is humored that my boots have names. One guy on the app sent me a text that said, "Keep the Boots On." Granted they are awesome boots, but I have not even spoke with this guy, so it came across as very presumptive. I did not reply.

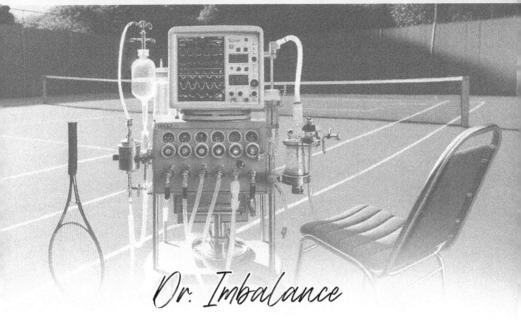

Dr. Imbalance

I was matched with another anesthesiologist who was rather handsome. I've often wondered if neurosurgeons, orthopedic surgeons, and anesthesiologists have to submit a headshot in order to specialize in their respective field.

This guy lives in Palm Desert and has never married and has no kids. We were talking, and I inquired about this. He admitted that he's a workaholic and spends his free time working out and playing tennis. Okay. Sounds like a good life.

He asked me if I read in detail the description of what he was looking for in a woman. I admitted that I had read it, but what I was hearing was that I didn't read between the lines. I inquired and asked specifically to what he was referring. He boldly said that he was looking to hook up only and did not want to commit to anyone. And he referred to himself in the third person as "doctor."

Next.

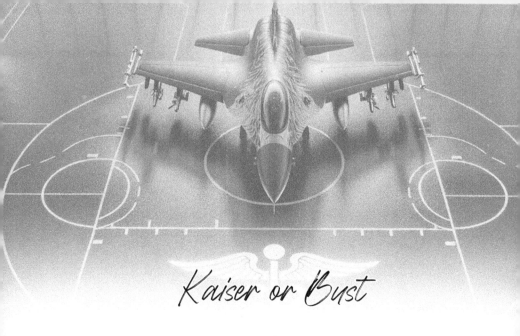

Kaiser or Bust

I was matched with a very handsome sports medicine doctor (you might be sensing a theme) who worked for Kaiser in the Inland Empire. He was a bright one who attended the Air Force Academy for undergrad where he played basketball for four years and Texas A & M for medicine. He was impressed that I was familiar with the term "Aggie."

He spent a good deal of time volunteering as a soccer coach, and he refereed games. It was a good referral source for his private practice in addition to Kaiser.

We spoke late into the evening one night, and we agreed that it would be fun to meet for dinner. He wasn't exactly geographically desirable especially in California where traffic is a nightmare. We planned to meet in the middle.

And then he disappeared. Ghost.

Sun Worshiper

This retiree was a stunner back in the day I'm sure and his photos were of years past. He loves to golf and ski and dance and play pickleball and good wine. Perfect. He lives in La Quinta, which is in the Palm Springs area, so it is again geographically undesirable, but he was willing to drive and meet me for dinner in Newport Beach. We were supposed to meet on a Sunday afternoon. He was willing to drive three hours each way for dinner. That's an impressive effort.

The day before, I was at some friends' house, and he was texting me about how excited he was to meet me in person. I was also excited. I've never seen such gorgeous blue eyes. He was out on the golf course that day with his buddies and he had a friend snap a picture of him. He was fit and dressed well. The problem was that he's had way too much sun and he looked older than my dad.

I know it sounds shallow, but I had to cancel. I felt bad about it, but I avoid the sun to protect my skin, and I just couldn't date him.

Please! No More Speedo Pics!

Matched again with another orthopedic surgeon who was an IronMan triathlete. I too have completed the IronMan, and it is a hard race to put it mildly.

He was in incredible shape, and he was a little older and certainly pushing my age limits, but he had put in the work to keep his physique in tip-top shape. Unfortunately, he sent me pictures of him posing in a speedo every day for weeks. I was having a hard time with my appetite after receiving these pictures. I stopped responding. I still get speedo pictures but not as often. Thank goodness.

Sagittarius

He was a marriage and family therapist who had recently relocated to San Diego from Tennessee. These days it is usually people relocating from California to Tennessee, so that caught my attention.

We spoke for a long time, and he was very interested in meeting in Solano Beach for a hike. It's very beautiful there, and that was appealing. But then he charged down horoscope alley and that was not quite so appealing. Don't get me wrong, there are some truths to astrologers predicting people's personal lives and describing personalities in general. But it is not a universal truth by which I live and die. For him, it was more important than liking similar activities. We were both Sagittarius. That meant that we were perfect for each other. I tend to think that opposites attract. Too much fire in one room can be an inferno.

He disagreed. I couldn't hang my hat on his date of birth, so we agreed not to hike.

Pickleball Champ

I should have guessed his age when he said that the last time he voted, it was for Ross Perot. He was educated at the US Air Force and then Stanford, so he wasn't a dummy. He was retired and played pickleball every day. He was rated a 4.5.

I play pickleball sometimes, and I am clearly not a 4.5. I'm probably a .5 on a good day. However, we agreed to meet in Laguna Beach and hike. I chose one of the hardest trails I know because he was slightly older than I was seeking. He was punctual and wore appropriate footwear. However, he looked old. Again, too much sun. He was in good shape and an excellent conversationalist. But he looked old, and despite his education, he rented a basement apartment in Newport Beach. Too many divorces? I'm not sure.

FORE!

He belongs to Marbella Country Club, so he's done something well with his life. This golf course is incredible. He likes to golf obviously, and we share the same faith, and he lives nearby. In fact, I can see his house from my backyard. He has had an amazing life full of accomplishments galore. He's owned a ranch in Montana near where I grew up skiing in Big Sky. He owns a company that is building a new dump in San Juan Capistrano. The rubbish business is a cash cow.

It sounds too good to be true. He loves to ski. He golfs a lot. He has time and money on his side. The problem is that he looks very old and overweight, and he has not taken good care of his physical health. He spends too much time at watering hole 19 after golf, and it shows.

Who Needs to be Divorced?

We agreed to meet at one of my favorite hiking trails near my home. Badlands Park Trail has a 180-degree view of the Pacific Ocean, and on a clear day, one can see from Palos Verdes to San Clemente Island near San Diego. I hike there often and it is a perfect one-hour hike if one doesn't have a lot of time. He lives inland Orange County and doesn't make it down to the coast often, so he's looking forward to trying something new. It's not a well-known trail as it is in a neighborhood, so I sent him a pin to the trailhead.

He showed up in his Tesla (this was a common theme), and he was decked out like we were climbing Mount Whitney. He had his rucksack and his camel for hydration and sensible sturdy Merrills. I was wearing running tights and a running shirt and tennis shoes. I was wearing my baseball hat and sunglasses.

He looked fifty pounds heavier than his picture. This guy had to have been 6'2" and weigh 260 pounds. I'm petite. His head was the size of a boulder, and he had squinty eyes. I'm grateful that one can do this hike in an hour, and after that, I was going to jog back to my car and skedaddle.

He was a decent conversationalist and a clever businessman and had invested well in real estate. We talked mostly about his work, which was fine.

I'd made a rookie mistake of not getting his last name before I met him, but I had let three people know where I was hiking, and I sent them his photo. At the end of the hike, I asked for his last name out of curiosity. He gave it to me.

He was a little handsy on the trail which made me uncomfortable, and he asked to come over to my house after. That was not happening.

When I got home, I Googled him. Married. Not even a divorce filing in the works. Simply a married guy looking for a side hustle.

Hair Sniffer

Common theme is that I strongly prefer meeting on a very public trail for a hike. There are a number of reasons for this strategy. I hike every day anyway, so why not kill two birds with one stone. And a hike can always be cut short if things are not going well. This hike was cut short. He told me that he is really into pheromones and that he wanted to sniff my hair to see if our pheromones aligned. Nope.

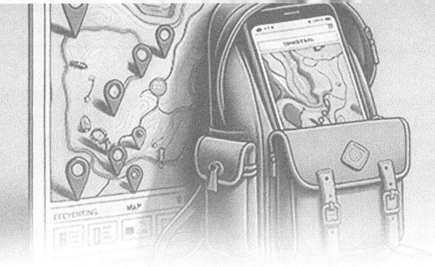

Tesla Troubles

It wasn't lost on me that so many of these guys drove a gray Tesla. It must be the thing the newly divorced guy drives. I was supposed to meet this man at the Badlands Park Trail and I was waiting for him. Once again, ever polite, I sent him a pin thinking that he was lost. It seemed slightly odd since he lived a few miles away in a town called Ladera Ranch.

He texted me on his iPad to explain that his phone was inadvertently in his son's backpack, and it was the key to his Tesla. He had the phone tracked on "Find My Phone," and he was watching it travel North on the I405 freeway. He had no way to start his car.

Again, an accommodating soul, I offered to drive to him and walk Ladera Ranch. He was grateful. I did in fact do this, but there just wasn't the energy I was hoping for. He was very nice and interesting and smart with a good job. But he had a young son and I'd already raised four.

Herkle Derkle

A Herkle Derkle is a Scottish term for someone who lingers in bed far too long. You probably already knew that. But this Herkle Derkle had told me on the phone that he never sleeps.

I went to Santa Clara University with him in 1983, but I did not know him. Based on yearbook photos, I was an idiot for not finding this preppy darling soccer player. But alas, I did not. And it's a small school.

Fast-forward the algorithm of the dating app, and he went to SCU and he was around my age, and he was a finance guy and he lived in the desert.

We spoke for hours about school and kids and life. He has a great personality. We share the same faith and love for our parents. He loves to ski. This is good.

I invited him to a Super Bowl party at my friend's house, but explained that I was going to mass before. He indicated that he hadn't been to mass in some time but was happy to accompany me to mass before the party, and he did.

He was surprised that the Catholics have changed up a bunch of their auditory responses. It is true. They have. And the Catholics don't like change. But once you get used to change, you don't really notice it much, and I've always loved change. It's new. It's hopefully a good thing.

I'm social, so when leaving mass, we ran into people and I introduced him. I was not sure of his label, but his name seemed to fit. I'm not into explaining myself. Then we went to the market to grab a few share items to take to the party. I paid. No problem. My friends. My party. I would have done this anyway.

We got to the party and needed to enter our initials on the squares for the pool, and I did so for him and me because I didn't tell him about the pool and I didn't want to get into the money game. I'd noticed that he was a short-arms deep-pockets guy at the grocery store.

I put his initial on nine squares and paid his nine dollars for his rental space on the board. I did the same for me. Us ladies take charge of the squares and the money and the pool and the payouts because we are an organized lot. The guys watch the game. Us gals only really care about the commercials.

At the end of a really good Super Bowl game, he won. Good for him!

He stayed at my house for two reasons. It's Super Bowl Sunday, so traffic was going to be awful, and it was going to be dangerous. And he lived two hours away.

The next morning, I have risen and have been working and cleaning and doing what I do. I went to check on him. He didn't imbibe at the party, so I know he's not hung over. He was all tucked in as a Herkle Derkle.

I'm a get shit done kind of gal.

Breadcrumbs

I've known him for over thirty years as we were in the same section in law school. Handsome and charming to say the very least, but in law school, he had a high school sweetheart and he was going to marry her. Fair enough. The electricity was hard to deny, but he was faithful and I was busy getting engaged to other guys that I didn't want to marry. It's pretty uncomfortable giving back rings to guys who could not afford the rings and to whom you've told that you don't see yourself as the marrying type. I'm fiercely independent and fearless. I was born that way. Nothing has ever seemed impossible to me.

I had referred Breadcrumbs many cases over the years as he was an excellent trial lawyer. We golfed together in bar association charity tournaments. He is a scratch golfer. I am not. But the rules require one woman in every foursome, and my motto was always to choose wisely. I chose him often, but not exclusively. Keep it mysterious. Guys apparently like this.

After my soulmate passed, I was pretty lonely. My kids seemed to be picking up speed in their lives, and it was a busy time with their school and sports and college essays and applications. We were busy. I'd gone back to work and was more interactive with friends and family. But I was lonely.

I reached out to him, and he immediately was thrilled to take me to dinner. We had a blast. He was like wearing old slippers that had been worn in perfectly. We fit.

He was divorced by now, and we were free to express our attraction and we did. It was incredible.

Ten years have passed, and we keep in touch only because of Breadcrumbs. Not mine. His.

He's Just Not That Into You

He seemed ideal. Ohio boy who wanted to go to Ohio State but chose otherwise for an athletic scholarship. I like guys who make sound financial choices.

We spoke for hours before we set a coffee and hike date. He chose a great place with a great vibe in Laguna. We met and talked and joked and laughed, and I felt like I was hanging with my brother.

We had a great hike as well regardless of the rain. I'm Wyoming, and he's Ohio, and weather is never the deciding factor.

We spoke of the fact that his divorce was amicable, but he would have preferred to have had kids.

I understand that. Raising my children has been the best privilege of my life.

I felt like our dinner ended well, and he walked me to my car. He gave me a grandpa peck. I asked for another kiss. He gave me another peck.

He was just not that into me.

Positive Attitude

He was the CEO of a publicly traded healthcare company and was very attractive. "Soft on the eyes" is what my grandmother would have said.

He needed to go to New York for the weekend for a wedding. He must have found a bride. I never heard from him again.

The Judge

No. Not me, but was linked to a guy who had relations to my first jury trial judge. I was a wreck, I suppose, but oddly, I'm fearless. I've never been afraid of anything (except losing your soulmate).

I figured I'd come full circle. I am a judge. He knew my first. The End.

Fire!

Retired fireman who was (of course) tall and handsome like all other firemen. We talked on the phone for hours about what we were looking for in a relationship and his non-negotiables mirrored mine. Trust: he's loyal and is slow to get in deep, but once it's a good fit, and there is deep friendship, he's committed. Integrity: imperfection is okay. Humanity is part of the deal. Passionate: we need to be attracted to one another in order to deeply love one another. Fitness: we need to be moving and doing and have a lot of fitness goals in common in order to fit. Travel: we need to see the world. It's a big world out there, and other cultures are worth learning about. Gratitude: we need to be grateful for the good things in our life and accept the things that are not what we had planned upon happening.

We met for a hike, and it was great. We walked and talked for hours. We planned to hike again, but he injured his foot, and so we met for coffee in Newport Coast at a place I love. We talked for hours overlooking the Pacific.

I broke my neck. I called him after my vacation in the ICU. He's compassionate about the gravity of the injury. We met for another hike, but this time he had to pick me up because I couldn't drive yet. We went to my favorite Badlands Park trail overlooking the Pacific. We had a lovely hike. He dropped me off and we hugged in the kitchen.

The End. I didn't hear from him again.

New Zealand

He's Swiss who lives nearby and is in program management. He's 55 and 6'2" and gorgeous. He's a Sagittarius (I don't hold it against him for posting this on the dating app). He loves to snowboard and watch hockey and loves to cook and drink wine.

We spoke for hours on the phone about life and places we wouldn't mind living. We both blurted out "New Zealand." We had so much in common. He's in upper management. Adult kids had left the nest. We had planned to go for a hike. And then I never heard from him again.

Let's Volley

He's sixty-six and a software executive and is Catholic. He loves to dance and golf and ski and go to concerts. He lives in Huntington Beach and plays volleyball competitively.

We were setting up a date to meet in the Back Bay to hike. I never heard from him again.

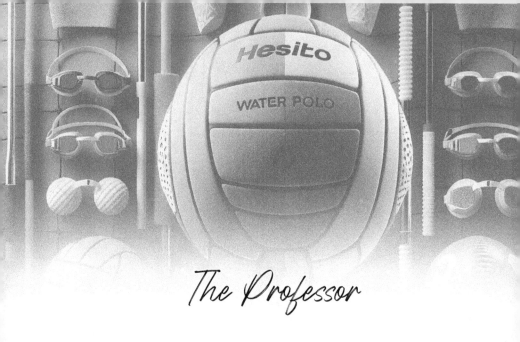

The Professor

He's a tech professor at Berkeley and smart and sexy nerdy *Big Bang Theory* kind of guy. He loves Portugal and Peru and water polo and swimming and is fit as a fiddle.

We were supposed to meet and have a weekend somewhere other than San Francico or LA.

But he never called back.

USC

He's a sixty-three-year-old USC grad who is a CEO of his tech company and gorgeous and Catholic. He loves football and basketball and cooking and dancing and boating and animals. He lives nearby in Long Beach.

We planned to meet in the middle and hike. But I never heard from him again.

Taco Tuesday

This handsome fit telecom exec who is sixty-five and 6'1" loves to ski, cook, dance, etc. He owns a boat and loves to sail. He loves animals. But he also loves tacos. There is nothing wrong with a taco. But he loves tacos. Taco Tuesday is his jam.

You may not like me after reading this sentence, but I don't love Mexican food. Cevice is my favorite. But filler tacos and burritos are not my thing.

It was a deal breaker for him.

You Are Under Arrest

Former LAPD. Highly respectable to me as I highly respect our law enforcement and I have not enjoyed the defund movement. He is a professor locally after retiring from from the LAPD, and he attended UDub (Washington) where a number of my friends attended. We talked for hours about his career and his future.

Not sure if he asked one question about me.

Porsche Meister

His pictures depict this very handsome man posing against his numerous porches like a model. He is a looker (my grandma would say that), but how many porches are in that garage? Jay Leno style? I don't know. He's retired CEO of this or that and he dabbles in this or that. He talks nonstop about this or that, and I lose interest. I've owned a 928 S4 and a 911. I know cars. I sold my latest 911 because I don't drive it like it should be driven. It should be driven hard and fast.

We are supposed to meet for drinks in Carlsbad. But I never heard from him again.

Let's Fly

He's a fifty-eight-year-old orthopedic surgeon in LA. Again he is stunning, and I'm convinced that all ortho dudes are headshot applicants. Smart. Fine. But gorgeous is what gets you into the residency and fellowship. It mirrors others, I know. And he's a pilot. Owns his own plane.

His kids are launched. His divorce was not good. He's a wounded bird. But he wants to try to find love again. He loves to ski and surf, and he is stunning and he's fifty-eight, so he is age appropriate.

He does not believe in God. Agnostic. I can't live with that.

This stable healthy gorgeous surgeon with a good career and great kids and he's geographically down the street is agnostic.

Terrified to Meet You

This man is a high-end founder of a surfing company in Laguna and worth a gazillion dollars and handsome and obviously smart and fit. We talked for hours.

He was terrified to date me. Who knows why?

Cubby Fan

Montana boy who loves nature and loves to ski and hike and camp. He rivals me in camping gear and I am an outdoor survivalist. Apparently this guy found me intimidating. I did the Nepal Annapurna.

The End despite the fact that I'm a Cubby Fan.

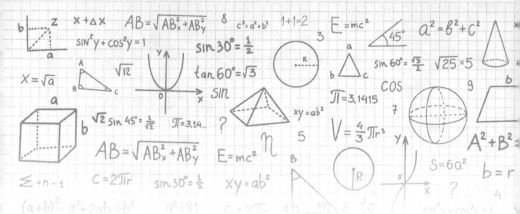

Outer Space

Chief Space Training and former Air Force cadet and pilot. Math wizard. Super interesting to converse with, but somethings was missing, and I couldn't put my finger on it. He would love to talk with me into the sunset, but he did not push to meet. Most guys push to meet. Not sure what was the deal.

9 AM

Aerospace engineer who is recently retired at age fifty-five and is lovely on the eyes. He lives in Palm Desert and golfs and skis and scuba dives and loves the mountains and camping and fishing.

He only responded at 9 AM every day. Precisely.

Like a BOT.

He was my mirror. But likely a BOT. Ugh. Story of my life.

Author's Note:

I didn't start out to date to write a nonfiction satire. I started out to start over. My husband in his class and infinite wisdom told me that he wished that I would find love again. He was a gentlemen's gentleman.

The odds of finding two soulmates in one lifetime must be around .00001. I'm a numbers gal. Let's figure out our odds. Play accordingly.

I took copious dating notes because it is a numbers game. I'm a listener.

I have a penchant for nicknames. It's a base form of entertainment. Nicknames hopefully will save me from a few scorned participants.

I am happy to report that I have quit the dating app game. It does not work for me. It will be organic and random and amazing. I've stopped looking. It will happen when it happens.

Printed in the USA
CPSIA information can be obtained
at www.ICGtesting.com
LVHW090212290724
786754LV00025B/183